DRAGONFLIES AND ALGEBRA

$$\pi$$

DENNIS TRUJILLO

FUTURECYCLE PRESS

www.futurecycle.org

Cover photo, dragonfly bokeh by Egor Kamelev; author photo by In Seon Lee; cover and interior book design by Diane Kistner; Chaparral Pro text, Trade Gothic and Agnostic Font titling

Library of Congress Control Number: 2020935021

Published by FutureCycle Press
Athens, Georgia, USA

ISBN 978-1-942371-86-1

For Steve Trujillo, 1956-1989

CONTENTS

III

I

π

FEAR OF TIGERS

So grandiose, the two Korean tiger
statues at the entrance to Shinheung College.
The extinct species carved from sandstone
as if they just padded down from Do-Bong
Mountain and leapt upon the pedestals.
They survey the campus grounds with eyes
like burned-out stars. Everyone loves them.
Passing coeds, in fashion dress, hope
the tigers' ambience brings good luck
on nursing exams. Professors and admin
workers bow to their native felines,
and foreign English teachers pose
for pictures with the tigers as if
they were mythological beasts.

But three find the statues grotesque—
the three white ducks in the pond
across the street behind the laurel hedge.
They're nervous and underweight.
Nighttime is the worst—the tigers' eyes
shine through the hedge like lanterns.

AT THE SCRAPYARD

Among rusted pipes and mangled metal
stand three telephone booths. They wait
like dinosaurs looking up at a sky

of dark ash. Inside, rigid metal cords hang
where phone books previously dangled
like bibles for the lost. These old servants

that once linked lives in exchange for coins
are no longer necessary to call home
from New York to say I made it. Not needed

to call friends to tell them what restaurant
to meet at. And not vital for calling a tow truck
because the Plymouth Duster is at a stoplight

with the hood up. The booths will soon be crushed
and sent to the smelter, their molten frames
cast into wire hangers, fry pans, and nails.

Hear the wistful voices as you hang
your jacket, the fried eggs full of gossip,
each nail with important news to tell.

DRAGONFLIES AND ALGEBRA

Today as I taught algebra
a throng of dragonflies hovered
at my classroom window—
gossamer wings gleamed
in autumn sun. Compound eyes
seized upon every number
and symbol on the board.

My students were watching
the clock, waiting to be rescued
by lunch, but the dragonflies
gazed with rapt attention—
iridescent bodies beamed
with interest. They shunned
the classrooms near mine,
English Lit and History,
as they sought only the cold light
of math and were unmoved
by Shakespeare's sonnets
and the Industrial Revolution.

The bell rang, and gel-haired
students vanished,
but the dragonflies remained
—wanting more.
I turned to the next lesson
and began explaining
exponential equations.

RITUAL OF SQUARE ROOTS

Around desert campfires, a clan of nomads
held sacred services to honor square roots
of numbers. Flushed with wild honey tea,

elders fell into a trance, and calculations
began. Desert wind buzzed with numbers.
Drawing with sticks in the sand, they squared

distances the caravan traveled by camel
each day—with simple ciphers for simple squares,
like six, from thirty-six kilometers.

More often, they met numbers like forty-one—
occult orphans of the sun—digits spinning
to infinity. These, they ciphered

fifty places past the decimal, with assistance
from ancient Babylonian tables.
They left scripts in the sand overnight,

trusting the moon to complete the task
of calculating immortal square roots
out to the sublime edge of absolute.

WHY I RUN IN THE RAIN

Because waterlogged shoes are a small price
to pay for the primal privilege of striding
through the wet harvest of clouds
with squinted eyes. Because dashing

through puddles with mud-splattered legs
shatters the stress of job deadlines
and the twenty-four-hour news channel.
Because a drizzle elicits golden

isolation—sane runners with soft spleens
take to treadmills—leaving trails open
for reckless hearts and startled
fat earthworms fleeing inundated tunnels.

Because the caress of a soft cotton towel
and a sip from a hot cup of tea
are the same bounty reserved for angels
after an ebullient run in the rain.

BE PRESENT WITH THE POSE

Ash-colored and lighter than dust,
a spider roamed the center
of the room where I wanted

to lay my purple yoga mat.
She wouldn't shoo when I flapped
the mat like a dark thundercloud—

stood her ground like a banyan tree.
I bent down, brought my face
inches from her bristly legs,

and blew soft puffs till she sailed
to rest along the wall. *There you go,*
I said, then spread the mat and began

soothing breaths. Moments later,
in shoulder stand, looking up
between my feet, I saw the spider

on the ceiling looking down
like a tiny guru. *There you go,*
she said, *let your breath flow.*

Be present with the pose.

SEARCHING FOR THE CLOUDED LEOPARD OF BHUTAN

Finding words for that fleeting urge
that brings forth a poem is like searching
for the clouded leopard of Bhutan.
In Himalayan foothills you think
you spot one creeping along a precipice,

but it's the shadow of a mountain hawk.
In the lush green south you're sure there's one
crouching under rhododendrons—
but it's a rotting log. From tangled brush
the blue-winged thrush laughs

at your futile venture. The guide points out
fresh tracks of the elusive cat
that lead to a cold blue lake, then vanish.
The scent of monsoon rain rises
from the east. You surrender—

head bowed like the weeping cypress.
You're folding your tent when a leopard
emerges from the fog-covered forest
and begins to nuzzle your hands.
The words come gushing out.

BLACK TEA FROM NEPAL

for Natasha

Cheeks still raw from her trek in Nepal,
my friend handed me a silver foil
of black tea—the kind Sherpas savor.

In the morning I poured boiling water
and watched the leaves unfurl
like black tulip petals. Aromas—

smoky sweetness, cardamom,
raven feathers. Texture smooth
as a celadon vase. A crisp taste—

undertones of apricot, cloves,
black diamonds—electrified
my tongue. I suddenly ached

for icy wind and snowy peaks
the way a planet without a sun
craves the muscled grip of gravity.

OKAME

Pisces Horoscope, Nov 4, 2011

You have something in common with the Japanese goddess
Okame. When the sun went into hiding and the world went
dark, it was Okame's wild dance that brought back the light.
Your exuberance will save the day.

—astrologer Holiday Mathis

The question that long gripped
my cranium like a shining scarab
is answered: Okame is my muse.

Once I thought my muse was a moth
flailing against the stained glass
of a church. Another time I was sure

it was a yellow leaf in the wind.
But, no, it's Okame, who charmed
the sun with her bare shoulders

and dance that shimmered
beneath a gossamer gown
of woven cherry blossoms.

O Okame—I will lacerate my chest
with a tattoo of your smiling face
so the lavender ink of your lips

seeps into my blood, bringing a gift
only a goddess can give—
the complete disrobing of my heart.

WOODEN BICYCLE

I ride a wooden bicycle,
carved from strong red oak.
The texture is coarse
with straight grain and a few
knots like dark oases rising
in a reddish-tan desert.

The chain is fabricated
from spruce, the same wood
used for crafting vintage violins.
As I swerve around corners,
it whirrs with a clear tone
equal to the finest *Stradivari*.

The handlebar horn of whittled
Ponderosa pine emits shrill
warning calls of frightened
woodland birds, and the tires,
shaped from black willow trunk,
leave resin tracks like clues
in a mystery novel.

It's dependable and solid
for transporting goods
home from the market,
but when I cycle
through its sylvan home,
sap begins to flow through its veins
and twigs emerge
from the dogwood pedals.
When I stop to rest,
it instantly shoots sinuous roots
deep into the forest floor.

RUNNING SEASONS

I.

Plumes of misty breath
and soft crunch of frozen snow—
winter morning run.

II.

Running on new spring
grass—pangs of joy shoot through my
veins like bright green light.

III.

Sultry summer day
running shirtless in clustered
hills—gilded with sweat.

IV.

Autumn's red branches
and sapphire sky—legs light as
white butterfly wings.

ROY G BIV

The colors of rainbows and all spectrums
of light reveal themselves in this order:
Red, Orange, Yellow, Green, Blue, Indigo, Violet.
I learned this pattern in seventh grade
from Mr. McNish. His voice had a slight tremble,
but I recall his words just as I recall
the reverence with which he handled
the glistening human skeleton that dangled
near the classroom door.

In eighth grade, Mr. Consonero brought order
and light to algebra with lucid demonstrations.
The rhythmic tapping of the white chalk
on the blackboard was a clarion call
to unravel the mystery of numbers.
Formulas I once feared became like
cheerful bellhops offering to carry my bags.

In high school, I ran cross-country under
Coach Pickering's care. He knew how
to develop endurance and speed in runners
the way a landscape artist knows how to paint
light unfurling over distant mountains.
He led our team to championships—but what
I remember most about running over hills, grass,
and muddy trails is an ethereal bliss so pure
it torched my heart.

Gentlemen, you are my heroes.

I hope I haven't let you down as I sit here
at my desk waiting for my third period algebra
students. My heart is still glowing
from a four-mile run this morning,
and the sun shines through the windows
in the full splendor of Roy G Biv.

TRICKED BY FAIRIES

On my walk to the train station,
I pass a stand of twisted pines
and spot two middle school students,

a boy and girl in their blue-gray
uniforms, hiding beneath the branches.
They're sharing a cigarette

and a carton of strawberry milk,
her hand cupping his elbow. Bright
and cute, their faces shine through

morning mist like polished
wooden dolls. *Say something,*
my inner voice demands.

It's your duty as a teacher.
I glance back, but they've vanished,
leaving a scent of primrose.

Around the trees, empty streets
and a badminton court: no place
to hide. Baffled, I turn away—

then laughter, taunting and playful,
drifts down like dew from high
in the tangled branches.

PREHISTORIC SHREW

Finally, after years of archeological
endeavor, a student finds on his tenth dig
the shinbone of a prehistoric shrew
encased in a layer of red shale
like a rusted cutlery utensil.
That's all—no skull, ribs, tail.

He expects a celebratory kiss
from his professor, with eyes
like Egyptian glyphs, and who led
the team to this desert passageway
near Qom—but she just frowns
and says, *Is that all there is?*

Turns out they were both wrong—
a Celtic scholar revealed
the artifact was a magic wand
from a primitive species of fairies
that flourished among the glaciers
of the early Pleistocene Period.

SHAMANS OF ATLANTIS

Shamans of Atlantis knew the secret
of night kites. They cut shapes
from stiff parchment and painted
cryptic symbols along the edges
with red paint. On summer nights
when the crickets were loudest,
they carried the kites to a grassy plain,
followed by throngs of Atlanteans
anxious to witness the phenomenon.
On a nod from the High Shaman,
the kites, unleashed, rose like
a flock of odd-shaped magical birds
powered only by moon glow.

The shamans never revealed
the secret of night kites to the people,
just as they never told them
the ultimate fate of their island—
the shifting tectonic plates,
the crashing waves—a prophecy
passed to the shamans by a crystal
quartz skull that spoke to them
in the hidden dialect of the stars.

REMNANTS OF DREAMS

On the first floor, a cardboard-covered path
leads out. Men with face masks
and dust-covered hats and clothes push

wheelbarrows laden with broken concrete
and wood like a colony of workers
at a tungsten mine on Mars.

The rubble is from the fifth floor,
once cramped student dorms now
being transformed into classrooms.

I ride up to see the work and tense
at the sound of dampened voices
and faint singing—all emanating

from the splintered walls, still dense
with dreams from hundreds
of students who slept there.

BLACK BUTTERFLY

At an outdoor restaurant
near a mountain temple in Korea,
two friends and I sat cross-legged—
protected from July heat by pines
and a cold running brook.

From the corner of my eye,
an enormous black butterfly
winged through the shadows
of rocks then disappeared.
Later it glided again into sight—
closer, like a bat in daylight
or a small bird pantomiming
to charm the mountain spirits.

Did you see that? But my friends
had not, so engrossed with soybean
pancakes and rice wine. Walking down
the mountain, I glimpsed it again—
a black phantom mirrored
on the brook's glass surface.

That night in a dream, mountain
spirits invited me to the temple.
The head monk served barley tea
and said the temple had been his home
since the Shilla Dynasty.

ROXBURY GARDEN REVISITED

Blue and pink sashes,
Criss-cross shoes,
Minna and Stella run out into the garden
To play at hoop.

Up and down the garden-paths they race,
In the yellow sunshine…

—from "A Roxbury Garden" by Amy Lowell

Sipping tea and scrolling through poems
online, I receive this sudden jolt
from a century ago—my daughter
Mina and my mom Stella racing
through a garden in criss-cross shoes—
as if it weren't already coincidence
enough that they share the same birthday.

I ponder this dreamlike picture
and think, yes, of course—were it
possible, my daughter and my mom
would have enjoyed playing hoop
together in the yellow sunshine.

That's my daughter in the blue sash—
Mom would have preferred the pink.

SACRIFICE

Ten per box—a fresh load of crabs
packed in sawdust on sale
at the Korean market. My wife,
overjoyed, mimics crab claws
with her fingers and thumbs
as she buys a box of distraught
crustaceans. At home she rinses
each, one by one, and places them
in the sink. From my desk
in the next room, I hear
their ancient claws click and clack
against the metal drain
like trapped miners. Four she chops
for soup. Six are frozen for later.
I write this poem in their honor.

$$\parallel$$

π

RUNNING LOG ENTRY

Aug 4, 1979: 8 miles steady on roads; hot;
stopped to turn over a turtle.

Once, when I was still single
and living in Killeen, Texas,
I was running along a road
and came upon a turtle
that had fallen off the curb
and was lying upside down—
legs waving like tattered leaves.

Arcane markings traced its under-shell
like a blueprint of the universe,
and I felt sure it was some
mystical creature. I carried it
like a baby across the street
and placed it on its feet
among wild grass and thistles.

Since then, every year on August 4
when I get out of bed and my feet
touch the floor, a momentary
rapture surges through my body
like light from an ancient star.

ARCHIPELAGO OF DEAD LANGUAGES

for Cathy V.

An archipelago of dead languages
exists on the foggy edge of modern
vocabulary and syntax. Opaque islands
rich in forgotten reserves of words,
myths, and recipes lie in the murky sea
of our collective memories like bees

preserved in amber. Sometimes,
shaken by epiphanies, we recall
a few words and phrases
from ancient glossaries—lists of plants
for age-old remedies, primal words
for *hunger, danger, ecstasy.*

BENEFICENCE OF DANDELIONS

Let's fall to our knees right now—
on lawns front and back—and beg
forgiveness from dandelions,
starry children of the sun.
We've pulled them whole
by their fleshy roots, trampled
their yellow faces, and sprayed
them with foul toxins—fools
to think we could expel
hallowed herbs from the garden.

All they did was offer us their soul.
Boil the yellow floret, stem, and root,
and you have tea that cleanses
the liver, banishes gallstones,
and stifles the fire of joint pain.
Their serrated leaves add glee
to dull lettuce salads,
and their white-winged seedlings
sail on the breath of angels.

GOURDS ON THE ROOF

I bought the old house with one aim—
to grow gourds on the flat-top roof.
I fashioned a framework with wood
and brown twine for the twisting vines

to climb. Yellow flowers flickered
like holy flames. A clutch of green
gourds peeked from beneath fan-shaped
leaves like jaguar cubs. They reached

the size of juggling clubs, sprouted
warts, and flaunted orange and white
stripes. Dried, they became waxy
instruments of magic. At night

they began to resonate inside
my dreams, revealing ancient secrets
of the Incas—techniques for terrace
gardening, tips on raising llamas.

THE GRASSHOPPERS SPEAK

In midday heat we wait in weeds
like chips of wood. In rain we shine
    like ceramic pots.

Our hops are short and jagged,
pulled by faint gravity of rocks,
and we envy not the brazen
    flight of wasps.

We delight in alfalfa and corn,
but in drought we'll eat tumbleweeds,
    gnaw fence posts.

Our tribe is prey to blue jays,
centipedes, skunks, and shrews—
a fate scripted in craggy grooves
    of oak trees.

Our compound eyes see every night sky
with bright swirls as in Van Gogh's
    Starry Night.

We've heard rumors of ice
    but cannot imagine it.

STRIDE FOR STRIDE

For a twinkling instant this winter
morning, I glimpsed an angel
running next to me. A holy being
matched me stride for stride along a path
   lined with frost-covered reeds.

Celestial energy crackled
like electricity—a halo
of sacred breath hovered. She was
evanescent on my periphery—
   there, but not there.

The encounter stayed with me
all day like a shivering diamond
in my mind—I imagined it as
the best way to be escorted
   into heaven sometime.

WINTER ORACLE

Evening drive on wintry back roads—
patches of snow reflect the sun's dying
radiance as if pink rose petals
            have fallen there.

Cedars in the distance pose like a choir
preparing to sing Handel's *Messiah*.

A brown horse stands outside a ramshackle barn
like a prophet who preaches each day is a miracle.

I lower the car window and let the cold air
            grant absolution.

OMNISCIENCE OF ABACUS BEADS

Clusters of stars you see at night
are abacus beads summing infinity.

Droplets of dew on peonies—
the chilled eggs of abacus beads.

Buddha bracelets serve as harnesses
for abacus beads in meditation.

An abacus bead tied to fishing line
makes an ideal anchor for a popsicle-stick ship.

A magpie looking into a mirror recognizes
itself because it has abacus beads for eyes.

Sound of someone washing dishes—
abacus beads washing onto a rocky shore.

The moon is a celestial kiln
where abacus beads are hardened.

Hailstones are abacus beads
enumerating purchases of clouds.

VERNACULAR OF TREES

Trees speak among themselves
in various dialects. Their voices
vibrate far outside the realm
of human ears, but wood ants sense
conversation in branches and bark.

Like people, they sometimes struggle
grasping accents from faraway places.
Giant kapok trees of the Amazon,
with sultry voices, can't follow
cold tongues of Canadian cedars.

Topics of discourse include the bliss
of photosynthesis, poetry of birds,
mathematics of stars. Every night,
when the sun sets like a pink rose
over the Pacific, ancient redwoods

on the north coast of California
chant hymns of praise to the void
of Creation. Bonsai trees in Japan
listen with joy and amazement
as the sun rises over the ocean.

RIDING THE BUS ON A RAINY DAY

Silver needles of rain
pelt fogged windows.
Umbrellas huddle,

then splash through crossings
like shoals of lustrous fish.
My lungs are refreshed

at each stop when
the door cranks open
to waves of cool mist.

The bus jostles down
streets of shiny cars
and pine trees dripping

like tents. I might just skip
my station—go around
again, like a child

riding a painted horse
on a carousel
made of clouds.

OBSERVATIONS ON THE SUBWAY

In warm weather we sit stilted
in the small islands of our seats,
separated like gourmet chocolates
in compartmented trays. We cross
our legs, guard our space, and suffer
headaches from the dizzying blend
of deodorants and perfumes.
We avoid eye contact with faces
across the aisle the way rotting tulip
          bulbs hide from the sun.

But in winter, padded coats
and thick clothes break down
the invisible barriers the way snow
melts on train tracks. Shoulders press
together. The mere turning
of a newspaper page causes
an elbow jab into a neighbor's
quilted ribs, but it's comforting—
this impromptu human contact.
The gates of our hearts unlatch.

ALL UNDER CONTROL

Pisces Horoscope, May 29, 2013:

You have it all under control, though you might
have to tell your stomach. Feeling a little anxious
about the future is a good sign that your plans
are the right size for you...

—astrologer Holiday Mathis

I've had it all under control ever since
I bought thick black socks with gold toes.
Now I roam the house with the clout
of a man with two wolverines for feet.

And my once anxious stomach
now views the future with the same
equanimity of an origami crane.

My plans are the right size—
I only want to someday travel
the secret spirals of angels.

BARBER COLLEGE ON UNION STREET

When we were boys and our burnished hair
grew wild, Dad would take my brothers
and me to the barber college on Union Street.
Haircuts were free on the last four chairs—
two on the left and two on the right. Apprentice
barbers honed the art of scissors and shears,
and we, sons of steel workers and farm laborers,

were the blank canvases. Wooden benches
in the center of the shop were smoothed
and polished over the years by squirming
blue-jeaned bottoms of boys waiting their turn.
No frills—combs soaking in jars of light blue
disinfectant were the only curios
worth contemplating. Our feet rose in unison,

like leaps of trained dolphins,
as push brooms swerved with heaps
of greasy hair. The doors closed long ago,
but I still recall the barber college
every time my graying hair needs a trim.
The lady who cuts my hair wonders
        at my joy in paying.

STRUMMING MY PAIN

*—In the winter of 1973, Roberta Flack
released the hit song "Killing Me Softly"*

Bundles of laundry lay on the stoops
for plebes to deliver to rooms
of upperclassmen. Returning from class,
I balanced my books and two bundles
and bounded up the metal staircase

of Company F4. Winter had arrived
at West Point, 1973. Soft snow blanched
the granite landscape. Delivering laundry
that cold day, I was struck motionless
in the hallway like one of the many

campus statues when I heard
"Killing Me Softly" from an upper-
classman's room. The mesmerizing voice
and melody transfixed my heart
the way whiteout in a forest

rivets the senses. For four minutes
I drank in the song that shimmered
like mist in the cavernous barracks
as if the universe somehow knew
it was the gift I needed most.

AFTERNOON RAIN

Afternoon rain weighs down
the heavy heads of sunflowers
and surprises walkers

in the park—clothes cling
like wet children,
and I think of the autumn day

I last saw your face,
thirty-five years ago on campus,
slender in your green dress,

hands like two quivering birds
on the curve of my spine
that morning we kissed.

Later, when you drove away
in your dad's car,
afternoon rain raked down

the last maple leaves in clusters—
I walked back to my room
through shallow red streams.

LEFT-HANDED SURPRISE

Left-handed students,
rare as palindrome
prime numbers
or lost time
in my math classroom
where numerals rhyme.

Like white buffalo,
a lonely few shared
my southpaw view
in twelve years
teaching at this school.

First day this year,
seventh grade:
three beaming girls
side-by-side
in the front row,
chatty as old ladies
at a bingo game
—all three lefties.

The one in the middle
called Stella,
my mom's name.

MUD PIES

The child makes luscious mud pies
of all shapes and sizes—brownies, fudge,
cupcakes—like an offering to the earth
from which her own clay body sprang.

She decorates them with daisy petals,
pine needles, sawdust, and places
her treasures on the patio to dry.
Then comes the storm.

It leaves a scattered galaxy
of base ingredients—a pattern
in which a clairvoyant could unwind
events that would befall her—

first prize in a middle school
piano recital, a ruptured spleen
from playing rugby for her college
team, a polished gold ring.

CRAYOLA THERAPY

Go ahead. Immerse yourself
in coloring a scene of a girl
flying a kite in the wind.
A choice might be sepia
for the sweater, the kite magenta.
Forest green will do for the tree
in the background. Open a box
of Crayola and bask in the vast
spectrum of soothing light
and childhood fragrance.
Let peace collect in your blood
like after a shot of peach schnapps.
And what of all that rudeness
on the road and at malls? It melts
when we become enthralled
coloring a picture of a sleeping dog
with collar and water bowl.
How about a chestnut dog,
plum collar, and cerulean bowl?
Periwinkle is the color of tension
floating out the window.

STOLEN RED KNEE PADS

They were blood red—
the wrestler's knee pads
my brother stole
from our high school
and gave to Mom
for relief while scrubbing
floors in our small house
made of wood, plaster,
and the smell of boiling beans.

I try to justify recompense:
my brothers and I donned
the school's red jersey
and ran cross-country
—racing along pine needle trails
and charging over grassy hills
like crazed warriors
to win for our school.
Doesn't this pay our dues?

Yet even today,
should the wrestling coach
or other official approach
any of our doorsteps
demanding remittance
for the stolen red knee pads,
we would sell our cars
and pawn our wives' jewelry
to pay the original price
        plus interest.

ORANGE CAKE

The dream summons me back
to my childhood home—summer
morning, sparrows flitting
outside the bedroom window,

Mom and Dad in the kitchen
sipping coffee and listening
to the radio. The open backdoor
invites a pillar of ancient light.

Dad has just returned from night shift
at the steel mill—his black lunch box
lies on the tabletop
like an omen. I strut in

and declare I want to bake
an orange cake. Mom smiles,
but Dad asks if I actually know how.
It's easy, I say, *just squish*

orange pulp and grate the peel
straight into the mix.
From the small oven,
an explosion of orange fragrance

drenches the kitchen. I glance
at my parents as their apparitions
fade like smoke from blown-out
     altar candles.

PHONE CALLS IN DREAMS

I've no problem with relatives,
both living and departed, visiting
my dreams like last night, when
Uncle Fred dropped by my cell
in a Mexican jail and brought
a corned-beef sandwich. Nor is it
a bother when childhood friends
enter my dreams and challenge me
to tetherball at our old elementary.
I even tolerate strangers—
wayward spirits who fly furtively
into my dreams like bats
feeding along a stream.

But phone calls in dreams haunt me—
crackly voices conveying messages
barely comprehensible, yet urgent.
I try to shout, *This is a dream,*
just deliver the message
in person! But my voice is paralyzed—
                    I can only listen.

I wake
and wonder if there is a dimension
where some spirits are trapped like fish
in small pools when tides recede.
To reach us they must place calls
through a benign galactic operator
who plugs them into a switchboard
of stars and says: *Your party*
is dreaming—you have one minute.

SPIDER BITE

Winter morning—fierce cold.
Passengers looked the same
as they shuffled on the subway train:
heavy coats of dark blue, gray, beige.

Then a vestige of light—a pretty Asian lady
half my age, long hair dyed blonde,
got on the train and stood next to my seat.
Her ruby fingernails matched

her shoulder purse as one hand grasped
the swinging triangular hand-strap
and the other roamed her smartphone
sending flickers down my spine.

My destination one stop away,
I stood and offered her my seat—
fool that I am. She gave me
a half-smile, and when she bent

to sit she pulled her long blonde locks
to the side to show me—a little below
and behind her left ear—a black spider
tattoo, intricate and spellbinding.

At my stop I lurched off the train
and clutched the hand rail—
tightness in my chest,
the whole world spinning.

III

π

THE RED SHIP HAS SUNK

—on the closing of Indianhead International School,
Uijeongbu, South Korea 5/29/2012

The Red Ship has sunk, I know—
I was a member of her harrowed crew.
The compass broke, the bulkheads cracked,
white waves crashed down, safe port out of grasp—
     and our passengers, the precious passengers,
     ages five to eighteen, cold hands gripping
     bags and books as they boarded rescue ships.

I embarked on the Red Ship thirteen years ago—
she listed to one side, the stern was low,
but her keel was reshaped, the hull mended,
till she ploughed the sea like a whale undaunted.
     And the crew, the magnificent crew,
     replaced again and again, kept the Red Ship on course
     as if sparks from the North Star burned in their hearts.

Aboard the Red Ship passengers studied and read—
history, chemistry, math, *Romeo and Juliet.*
They wrote English papers and painted
portraits of their own faces.
     The orchestra performed Mozart concertos, the choir
     sang Christmas carols, and once at a spring talent show,
     six girls danced to the Beach Boys' *Kokomo.*

Once a year the Red Ship came to port and dropped anchor—
there a group of passengers lighted ashore.
Wearing black robes and tears, they bid us farewell
like a swarm of black butterflies. I was on deck—I saw it all.
     The Red Ship has sunk—help me spread the word:
     No more lessons and taking attendance,
     now the hallways are dark, the bell silent.

MY GRAY SWEAT SUIT FROM JCPENNEY

is a cocoon lined with angel hair.
Slipping it on after work soothes
like soaking in a chamomile bath

while listening to Brahms. My gray
ensemble of fog lightens my bones
when I run, as if loping through glens

in the clouds, and my silver chrysalis
is a sedative on frigid nights
when iced branches crack in the darkness.

It's my granite cloak, the husk shielding
my tear-shaped heart. If today my life
crashes and I must leave my tiny house,

I will make a peanut-butter sandwich
with last scraps of bread, drape myself
in my gray sweat suit from JCPenney,

and walk out the door, impressed
by how Heaven holds the world close
like a baby wrapped in gray mist.

METEORITE WINE

A vintner in Chile is making wine with a 4.5 billion-year-old
meteorite in the bottom of the fermentation barrel.

—*The Drinks Business, 1/12/2012*

Let's all say thank you to the ancient traveler
from the asteroid belt, stone flag of creation,
which fell like a flaming bird
into the Atacama Desert and now emits

splinters of the cosmos into meteorite wine.
Come, toast with tinkling glasses high
and let the primordial dust collect
like halos in our blood. Listen closely—

humming of angels in every glass.
Taste the fiery kiss of eternity
with each sip. Can't you see? It's God's
signature witnessed before, only fleetingly

as thunder in the desert, a baby's laugh,
red splash of two cardinals on a frozen
clothesline. Secrets of planets, sun,
and life—all bottled now in meteorite wine.

CIGAR BOXES

Fragrant boxes about the size
of a college dictionary—

lingering scents of vanilla,
coffee, oak, and cherry.

Empty boxes of *Dutch Masters,*
White Owl, Muriel, and *Don Rey*

Dad carried home from the bar
where for a nickel you could twist

the handle and get a handful
of red and white pistachios.

Sweet-scented boxes passed to me
and my brothers as treasure chests

for gallant green army men,
marbles, magnets, plastic cars,

jacks, jawbreakers, *Old Maid* cards,
pine nuts, pencils, and folded notes

from skinny-legged grade school girls
and, later, used as trophy cases

for medals won in high school
track and cross-country races.

My wish for the world is that
everyone receives a cigar box

of his or her chosen aroma
and therein places treasures—

a nice pen, photos of friends,
an interesting green stamp.

GIFT FROM A GARDEN GNOME

Low clouds pass like an unbroken bolt
of corrugated cloth—dark enough
for the garden gnome to think it's night.

From the living room window, I watch
his clay body come alive among
the hollyhocks. With stuttered steps

he inspects the backyard like Earth's
curator. He squints at mushrooms
along the edge of the compost heap

and stuffs a few beneath his red cap.
A shed snakeskin in the onion patch
receives his scrutiny. He looks up

and sees me, his gleaming eyes
like black onyx, and waves his pipe
in greeting. Clouds scatter.

The gnome stiffens back at his spot.
I venture out and find a swarm
of rare butterflies and melons—
twice normal size and ripe.

STUNNED

Her small hands flitted
like two hummingbirds
as she handed me the essentials
and explained the procedure—
milk carton with top cut off,
add a measure of soil,
poke a hole with your finger,
drop in a shiny bean,
cover, add water,
place in the sun and it will grow.

This was her first-grade Earth Day
project at our school. I followed
her instructions—placed my guest
on my classroom windowsill
where the sun lingers daily.
I went about my normal routine
and, a few days later, happened
to glance at my visitor. Abruptly,
and without any help from me,
it had sprouted—

a leaf, like a green crab claw,
poked upward through the dark loam.
I was stunned, as if a shroud
had been ripped from my eyes.

ODE TO VEINS ON TOP OF MY FEET

Blue canals
of the heart
crisscross
and connect
on top
of my feet
like the sacred roads
of the Maya
in Yucatán
or like terraced
rice paddies
in the Orient.
They've streamed
every drop
of my blood
from the day
I was born,
and they flow
with equal aplomb
—whether I sleep,
run in the rain,
or push
a laughing child
on a merry-go-round.

MEMORIES OF WILDFLECKEN

It unfurls like an ancient tapestry—
the town of Wildflecken in the mountains
of Bavaria where I soldiered in 1977.

Our camp huddled on a hillside
above the town like a sentry in the snow.
We maneuvered in armored vehicles

that belched exhaust, pungent and black
as dragon breath. At night we bivouacked
in starless forests where frost formed runes

on trees and dreams were pierced
by high-pitched songs of medieval spirits.
After weeks of training in drifts and ripples

of snow, I shed my boots and exposed
chilblains stippled on my toes—
crimson trophies from the god of ice.

On the first glow of spring, I walked amidst
the pine forests that embrace Wildflecken.
At a clearing, the sun bade me lie

on the spongy earth, my folded jacket a pillow.
As I gazed at the cobalt sky, I could feel
the hoary ghosts of winter, hidden

deep in the chambers of my bones,
surrender to the sun's strident commands—
their wispy arms held high.

MADE IN HEAVEN

I'm riding the bus, listless, looking
at storefronts, cars, pedestrians—
my eyes dull as a parrot that's been
in a pet shop window for way too long.
Thoughts on what to do when I get home:
Online chess? Discovery Channel?
Bowl of chili? At a stop near the park
I see a homeless man, face tanned
brown as a chestnut, sitting
on a bench with pant legs rolled up
revealing dirt-crusted feet stuffed
in sandals. His cap has the phrase—
Made in Heaven. He raises his eyes
and looks at me. Pure light pours
from his eyes into mine, burning.
In my mind, a campfire is lit. I sit
on a log sharing hard-crusted bread
and a bottle of wine with strangers.

RED MOWER

Oh, I was much younger then, my dear
daughter still a toddler. We lived
in army quarters at Fort Lewis,
and of course the army expects
you'll keep the grass cut short as your hair.
So at a mega home supply center,
I said, *I'll take the red mower,*
and two burly men plopped
a coffin-sized box onto the bed
of my Nissan pickup. At home
I slit the lid, and a spasm crackled
down my neck—it seemed more like a kit
to construct a robotic insect.
I said, *Mama, take the baby*
to the Tacoma Mall. I have a project
that requires the focus of bees.
Allen wrench, valves, ratchets—
none of these easy for a left-handed
guy like me. But I knuckled down,
poured myself into the job as if
it were the Apollo Lunar Lander.
When wife and baby came home,
the grass was cut short with machine
precision, and I was sitting
on the concrete floor of the carport
drinking Redhook amber ale.
The mower loomed in the backyard
like a giant red ant from Mars.

MY HEART SPROUTS WINGS

Running along an exercise trail,
I chanced upon a pigeon flapping
its wounded wing in a patch
of purple heather. It made me think

of an escaped convict in shackles.
I felt for the bird with mottled
gray-and-white feathers—hoped
it might recuperate and join

its mates perched on girders
beneath the faded concrete bridge.
Next day, still there. Two others
kept company like sentries

at a queen's chambers. The third day
it rained. The injured bird and its
companions were gone—don't know
if it flew away or if it died.

Now every time I run past
that spot, my heart sprouts wings.

FIELD OF ONIONS

One morning, as he walked
through a field of onions,
a man heard far-off music gliding
through the air with the beauty
of sparkling rare jewels, the notes
fleeting as they echoed along
the rickety wooden fence.

A great solar wind blowing
across Venus had drawn music
from the oval mouths of volcanoes
and carried it across the heavens
to resonate in summer mist
above the furrowed field.

Old now, the smell of onions
still reminds him—the red sun
rising, the thrum of Venusian
music burnishing his heart
like the breath of fiery angels.

SEVEN SCARVES

I keep them rolled in a drawer
like a knitted rainbow—the seven
scarves my students gave me
during my thirteen-year tenure
teaching math at a school
in Uijeongbu. I always resisted,
saying, *Please, it isn't necessary,*
but in Korea gifts to teachers
are customary. There was also
green tea, rice cakes, acorn jelly,
and ginseng candy. Each time
presented with a scarf, I wore it
all winter long like a glowing
Olympic medal, adding brio
to my dull beige coat.
One Lunar New Year,
Jessica gave me a burgundy
scarf with fringe and Hae-Ri,
a knitted green one. I took turns
wearing them, wanting both girls
with gleeful giggles to stay
motivated in my math class.
That was years ago—
now each winter when I open
the drawer, memories startle me
like early spring tulips.

VOICES

Gnomes or nymphs, I wondered,
as anomalous voices
wobbled in the shallows
of the night. I fumbled
my way to the living room,
half expecting to encounter
nature spirits lolling
cross-legged on the couch
and reading old editions
of *National Geographic*
scattered on the coffee table.

Instead, strands of starlight
murmured through the branches
of the ginkgo tree outside
my window in a language
only fairies and fireflies
        could unravel.

SUNRISE ALTAR

Like Noah's impulse to build an ark,
I woke with a glint in my heart

and drove to Home Depot to buy
a wooden trellis and two

packets of morning glory seeds—
small and black like the eyes of bees.

The sun and I partnered for weeks,
performed our duties like fervent monks—

me with silver mists of water,
the sun with golden buckets of light.

Cheerful vines with heart-shaped leaves
soon twined the trellis green. And when

funnel-shaped blooms burst into color—
violet, crimson, pink, white, and blue,

the trellis sparkled like a sunrise altar
that could be seen from the farthest star.

FRESH FOOTPRINTS ON THE WHITENED STREETS

Stepping out the door, silence
of fresh snow jolts my senses
like a windowpane shattering
without sound. I set out

on my run—the *swish-swish*
of my stride tracing fresh footprints
on the whitened streets. The world
is shuttered and asleep.

Streetlights feathered with snow
bow like mute swans clenching
shiny pearls in their bills. Stillness
and the meditative *swish-swish*

free my spirit. For a few moments
I float above the frosted trees
and look down at my clay body
loping across the white labyrinth.

AT MOMENTS PREORDAINED

To the over-antsy workers
responsible for sweeping
autumn leaves along the streets
of Dongducheon City: Please
stop whacking the branches
with long poles to complete your task
in a hurry as if eradicating
a medieval scourge. Left alone,
yellow ginkgoes and red maples
release their leaves at moments
preordained by the same algorithms
that tell gray whales when to migrate
and volcanoes when to boil.

WHERE ANGELS VACATION

Sign outside the subway entrance:
Watch Out for Falling Icicles.
My spine, itself a chiseled braid
of ice, quivers. I can't believe
winter would be so cruel as to drop
a clouded spike onto someone's skull
or shoulder. Early this morning
when I ran near the river, moonlight
lit the snow bright as a winter island
where angels vacation.

MORSE CODE OF THE STARS

Stars have a Morse code with which
they chronicle their existence.
Dashes and dots leap across space

with gossip of the galaxies.
They love to relate anecdotes
about their planets the way Earth parents

talk about their kids: *My third one*
just started supporting life,
or, *The one a hundred million miles*

away is so stressed—I'm afraid
she's going to blow herself up.
Mostly, though, they use Morse code

to recite poems of universal wisdom—
like how eternity lasts only a moment
and a moment lasts for all eternity,

and how there is only one moment.

NOTE

The horoscopes appearing at the beginning of the poems "Okame" and "All Under Control" appeared in the *Pacific Stars and Stripes* newspaper on Nov 4, 2011, and May 29, 2013, respectively. They are the work of syndicated astrologer Holiday Mathis.

π

ACKNOWLEDGMENTS

The author is grateful to the editors of the following publications in which some of the poems in this book first appeared.

3Elements Review: "Fresh Footprints on the Whitened Streets"
Agave: "Running Seasons"
Anima Poetry: "Omniscience of Abacus Beads"
Ascent: "Phone Calls in Dreams"
Atlanta Review: "At the Scrapyard"
Bewildering Stories: "Field of Onions," "Shamans of Atlantis"
Blast Furnace: "Searching for the Clouded Leopard of Bhutan"
Chanterelle's Notebook: "Okame"
Edge: "Gourds on the Roof," "My Gray Sweat Suit from JCPenney"
Eye on Life: "Afternoon Rain," "Wooden Bicycle," "Memories of
    Wildflecken"
Highland Park Poetry: "Black Butterfly"
KYSO Flash: "Spider Bite," "Vernacular of Trees"
The Old Red Kimono: "Stolen Red Knee Pads"
The Quotable: "Sacrifice"
Sacred Cow Magazine: "Made in Heaven," "Observations on the Subway"
Snapdragon—A Journal of Art and Healing: "Meteorite Wine"
Tales of the Talisman: "Voices"
Talking River: "Black Tea from Nepal"
THEMA: "Left-Handed Surprise"
Third Wednesday: "Barber College on Union Street"
Three Drops from a Cauldron: "Tricked by Fairies," "Gift from a Garden
    Gnome," "Prehistoric Shrew," "Winter Oracle"
Wild Goose Poetry Review: "Dragonflies and Algebra," "Why I Run in
    the Rain"
Young Ravens Literary Review: "Morse Code of the Stars," "Strumming
    My Pain"
Your Daily Poem: "At Moments Preordained," "Be Present with the
    Pose," "Crayola Therapy," "Fear of Tigers," "Riding the Bus on a
    Rainy Day"

"Running Log Entry" appeared in *The Best of Kindness II Anthology* (Origami Poems Project, 2017).

"Sunrise Altar" appeared in *Poetry of Flowers Anthology* (Lost Tower Publications, 2016).

"Spider Bite" was nominated for a Pushcart Prize in 2016 by the editor of *KYSO Flash,* Clare MacQueen.

The author also extends his deep appreciation to April Ossmann (poet, teacher, and editor) for her valuable assistance with the initial draft of this collection and to Alvin J. Green (poet, teacher, and soldier) for providing insightful feedback to an early version of the manuscript. Love and thanks also to family, friends, and sometimes kind strangers who offered encouragement along the way.

ABOUT FUTURECYCLE PRESS

FutureCycle Press is dedicated to publishing lasting English-language poetry books, chapbooks, and anthologies in both print-on-demand and Kindle ebook formats. Founded in 2007 by long-time independent editor/publishers and partners Diane Kistner and Robert S. King, the press incorporated as a nonprofit in 2012. A number of our editors are distinguished poets and writers in their own right, and we have been actively involved in the small press movement going back to the early seventies.

The FutureCycle Poetry Book Prize and honorarium is awarded annually for the best full-length volume of poetry we publish in a calendar year. Introduced in 2013, our Good Works projects are anthologies devoted to issues of universal significance, with all proceeds donated to a related worthy cause. Our Selected Poems series highlights contemporary poets with a substantial body of work to their credit; with this series we strive to resurrect work that has had limited distribution and is now out of print.

We are dedicated to giving all of the authors we publish the care their work deserves, making our catalog of titles the most diverse and distinguished it can be, and paying forward any earnings to fund more great books.

We've learned a few things about independent publishing over the years. We've also evolved a unique, resilient publishing model that allows us to focus mainly on vetting and preserving for posterity poetry collections of exceptional quality without becoming overwhelmed with bookkeeping and mailing, fundraising activities, or taxing editorial and production "bubbles." To find out more about what we are doing, come see us at www.futurecycle.org.

THE FUTURECYCLE POETRY BOOK PRIZE

All full-length volumes of poetry published by FutureCycle Press in a given calendar year are considered for the annual FutureCycle Poetry Book Prize. This allows us to consider each submission on its own merits, outside of the context of a contest. Too, the judges see the finished book, which will have benefitted from the beautiful book design and strong editorial gloss we are famous for.

The book ranked the best in judging is announced as the prize-winner in the subsequent year. There is no fixed monetary award; instead, the winning poet receives an honorarium of 20% of the total net royalties from all poetry books and chapbooks the press sold online in the year the winning book was published. The winner is also accorded the honor of being on the panel of judges for the next year's competition; all judges receive copies of all contending books to keep for their personal library.

Made in the USA
Coppell, TX
19 April 2020